NETWORK MARKETING

How It Really Works

And

How It Can Work For You

by
John & Hazel Stephen

To Margaret

[handwritten inscription]

Dedication

We dedicate this book to

All the Leaders who inspired, educated and motivated
us in the early years - we thank you for opening
our eyes to what this incredible industry
can give to anyone
who wants it badly enough.

To the Leaders with whom we associate today
who are also our friends - we thank you for
all your guidance,
encouragement and wisdom.

Acknowledgements

To the team of people we have worked with over the years.
We have won together, we have lost together,
we have struggled together, we have triumphed together,
and together we will continue to ride it to new heights.

To Angus Whitson for his skill with words
and dedication to our deadline,
and his patience with John.

To Alex Owens for her brilliant cartoons.

Contents

Foreword

This book is one of those rarities in our industry - a book written by people who are actually building a successful Network Marketing business!

Many of "How to Succeed in NWM" books are quite clearly written by people who did not succeed in our industry and so decided to write a book instead.

John and Hazel Stephen are .....one of the genuine rags to riches stories ..... become incredibly successful in NWM and in the field of personal development ..... a genius for simple, plain communication. The simplicity of their approach is at the core of their success.

Follow the information in this book and it does not matter what your background, experience or personal abilities are - you will be successful.

Simplicity is the key and it does not come any more straightforward than this.

Chris Mason-Paull
Co-founder of MIB Group

Chapter 1

How We Got Started

Since 1990 we have both worked full-time in the Network Marketing industry. We are still actively running the business which we set up together, and we work together in it every day. We absolutely love what we do and still have tremendous passion for the industry and the company which we have represented since 1995.

At the same time as we have been successfully achieving for ourselves and our family, we have been helping others to achieve and succeed for themselves. This is why we continue to be so active in our business today.

In this chapter we tell you who we are and how we got involved in this fantastic industry. We will take you over the hurdles we, and others, have experienced on our journeys to success.

John takes up the story. I came out of an industry I thought I would work in all my life. Hailing as I do from the northeast of Scotland, it was the local and family tradition of deep-sea fishing. I had the courage and foresight to leave that industry as it started its rapid decline.

When we were introduced to network marketing I was working on a self-employed basis for a neighbour who owned a small company. Hazel had just had our second child who was three months old at the time, and our eldest child was only two years old. She also helped out at her old office, doing the accounts when they were short-staffed.

The Introduction

In 1990 a good friend called in to see us, as he often did when he was in our area. He had left the fishing industry some years previously and had joined the insurance industry.

He knew that since I had left the fishing I was wanting to change direction too, and he had been looking out for an opportunity for me on shore where I could make serious money. I could have joined him in the insurance business but I had no interest or inclination to do so. There were too many examinations and too much paperwork involved, and it was not a direction I wanted to take.

He came up with some fairly far-fetched business ideas that he was sure would make our fortune. One was selling revolving tables for fishing boats, to process fish onboard while at sea. As the crew were being tossed about by the rough seas, they would get dizzy trying to catch fish as they whirled round the revolving table! Not such a good idea. Another suggestion was home-based salmon farming in the tiny back garden of our two bedroom semi-detached house. Environmental issues apart, what would our neighbours have said?

We were much more excited and intrigued by a business idea which our friend described to us as MLM (which of course stands for Multi Level Marketing). He was very enthusiastic about MLM and felt it had a lot of potential for us. He told us only that it involved retailing products and if we wanted to introduce other people to the programme we would be paid an over-ride on everything they did. The aim was to build a small team.

Our friend asked if he could give our telephone number to a client of his, a sheep farmer in the remote Shetland Islands, which lie between Scotland and Norway, who could tell us much more about this business opportunity.

The Phone Calls

The Shetland farmer had a flock of 900 sheep, but he was extremely enthusiastic about his introduction to MLM, and we had several encouraging phone conversations with him. We agreed with him that, because of the distance involved, the man who had introduced him to the business of MLM, a part-time evangelist who lived more locally, should call us and tell us more.

Another phone call, and a date and time were set for the following week.

The Appointment

Hazel continues the tale. Can you imagine what we were thinking? MLM, sheep farmer, part-time evangelist, what was coming next? I tidied the house and shipped the children off to their grandparents, and we waited in anticipation for the man who had all the answers to this business called MLM.

He arrived and set up his slide projector in our lounge and proceeded to explain MLM. Although at that point we did not for a moment imagine that this was where our future lay …… the rest you might say is history!

On the fourth of July 1990 John and I took the plunge and made the decision to become distributors for an international network marketing company. We only wanted to move enough products to earn some extra money, and that day we could never have imagined how our lives would unfold.

DECISIONS

No one ever makes a right decision
At the time of taking a decision you do not know if it is a right or wrong one.

What we totally believe is, once we take a decision we must commit to it and work at it, making sure it becomes the right decision.

The First 3 Months

We were successful during this time, retailing extremely well and earning the extra income we had hoped for.

Our sponsor (the person who introduced us to the programme) looked after us well, communicating regularly and encouraging us to attend open nights and training events to learn more about the business of Multi Level Marketing. We asked ourselves - "What is there to learn?" We had good results and were more than happy with the extra income.

A training meeting in Glasgow, which involved an overnight stay, seemed an ideal opportunity for Hazel to do some city shopping without the children. Truth to tell, our intention was to slip into the meeting, sit at the back, and slip out again before anyone spoke to us. It seems incredible now, but the fact that the meeting was led by one of the company's top earners, who would share his knowledge and experience with us, was a secondary consideration.

When we arrived the room was packed and only two seats were left in the middle of the front row!

Our First Training

We expected there would be only a handful of people there, like ourselves, a bit down on their luck. Surprisingly, there were all types – students, lorry drivers, business people, single parents – all ages and backgrounds.
The Top Earner was introduced to the music of Tina Turner and 'Simply the Best'. Throughout his lively presentation we felt that we were the only people in the room he was talking

to. The high spot came when a copy of his latest bonus cheque flashed up on the screen. To the gasps of the audience, he revealed to us how much he had earned the previous month, saying –

"You too can have a cheque like this if you are willing to be totally teachable and learn our system"

That bonus cheque was more for a month than some people earned in a year. When he repeated his statement it seemed intended only for us.

It was the moment of our conversion; we realised there was so much more to MLM than we had initially believed. We couldn't sleep that night, we didn't even go shopping next day. All we wanted was to return home to start building our own team, and start carving out our future.

We had seen the evidence
We had experienced the emotion
We had felt the excitement

To this day we both recall the statement that transformed our lives

"You too can have a cheque like this if you are willing to be totally teachable and learn our system"

We knew we had a massive amount to learn about the concept of MLM, about the industry we had joined, the 'How to's of team building – the list was endless. We went everywhere and anywhere to listen to people who were already making it happen.

A day's training in London would cost us more than we could afford. But we knew we could not afford NOT to be there if we wanted the big rewards. It was not a matter of choice and we went to London. We both still have our notes from that training day.

Recommended reading, listening to training tapes, attending training sessions – we were sponges for knowledge. And we applied what we learnt straight away, putting everything into practice as soon as possible. We accepted total responsibility for our own education because we believed what we were told in training, that –

'The quicker you learn the quicker you earn'

Personal education and development became part of our mission; and we still work on that principle today. No one should ever stop learning. Learning consistently and developing as a person are vital to making a success of your network marketing business.

As a business, a nd as your role in that business,
develops you must   keep moving forward.

Ye Olde saying:

'The more you learn the more you earn'

and

'You can earn while you learn'

Mistakes and Lessons in the early days

Mistake no. 1

We thought – What was there to learn?

This is a common problem when starting in this industry. It is also a common pitfall for people who have attended only a few meetings and training sessions, and think they know everything. What is there to learn? - The system!

We will dedicate a full chapter to each part of the system which we and our successful team members use.

Lesson no .1

As this book unfolds you will discover how our lives have changed. And we'll tell you some of the good things, and the bad, that have happened to people in the industry, past and present.

When you become part of something new, you have so much to learn. You have skills and experience to contribute, but the most important contribution to success in your new career will be your ability to become teachable. To take the knowledge and apply it effectively.

Mistake no. 2

Some people, seeing the big rewards achievable in this industry, say 'Oh Wow!' Never believing they will earn such an amount or achieve the same.

Lesson no. 2

We didn't make this mistake. Our attitude wasn't just, 'Oh Wow!' – it was

"Oh Wow, show us how!"

Chapter 2

Why?

In this chapter we share with you WHY we took the bull by the horns and invested our future in this industry. And some of the reasons WHY other people we know have done the same. The nature of the industry allows you to choose WHY you join it, and to choose the level of income which you have set your heart on.

When asked 'WHY' they chose Network Marketing, some people have specific reasons such as providing for the holiday of a lifetime; buying a new car or their dream home; paying for children's education; topping-up pensions. There are normal, everyday people looking for a new challenge, while others seek a career change which gives them control of their lives and future.

Some, already in full-time employment, want to supplement their employed income with part-time work. Often the attraction is in response to the fast changing world we live in, starting part-time to provide security for themselves and their family against likely or unforeseen redundancy. Others are motivated by the quality of the products, or see the potential that the concept and the Marketing Plan offers them. The vast majority of people who become distributors do so, ultimately, for financial reasons.

In the early days of our networking career we used to think it was inspiration or desperation that motivated us. We know now that it was a combination of factors, but the one overriding factor was we had a very, very strong 'WHY'

'WHY' for us was to pay off huge debts, to own a house again, to take our children on holiday, to rebuild our lifestyle and provide for our children's future.

John often starts his training events and seminars with these statements:

> The great organisations of the world, the great lives of history have been built on the answer to
>
> WHY
>
> You can teach someone to do a task, but that doesn't ensure they will do it.
> Help them discover
>
> WHY
>
> And they will learn in spite of all the obstacles.
> The key is not to know HOW but
>
> WHY

What's YOUR 'Why'

In every business the first thing you need is a strong – 'WHY'
To make any serious lasting impression you must find, what
for you, is your own strong 'WHY'
It's about discovering your reasons, your goals; and helping
your team find their own reasons 'WHY'
Everybody's 'WHY' is different.

> Your 'WHY' will get you out of bed in the morning
> Your 'WHY' will keep you focused
> Your 'WHY' will drive your business forward,
> determining the speed you build
> your network marketing business

In John's book 'Where does it all START?' there is a whole
chapter devoted to finding your 'Drivers' or your 'Reasons
Why'. Reading this chapter will help you discover your
strong 'WHY'

Your 'WHY' will continually evolve as you and your
business grow. If you have had your own networking
business for some time, and are failing to progress – it may
be time to revisit your 'WHY'. To discover what it is you
really want and become the person who deserves to reach
their goal. What you want today may be different from what
you wanted at the outset.

Grasping the Concept

Network marketing is not a job – it is your business, and
business can be tough. The moment you become involved
with network marketing you become MD (Managing

Director) of your very own business. This may sound alarming, may even put some people off. But how you deal with this reality will determine how successful you become.

You may start your business to supplement your current income, satisfied with earning £50-£60 (or euros or dollars) per week. But we guarantee that if you grasp the network marketing concept unreservedly, your ideas will change and you will discover your strong 'WHY'

A prime example is an ex long-distance lorry driver who joined us just to supplement his income. He is now one of our best team leaders, working full-time, earning more and enjoying a better lifestyle than he ever dreamt of. How he viewed the industry, and his potential within it, helped him find his strong 'WHY'. He saw the potential he had not seen in the early days, and he thought to himself – "WHY not me?"

You need a strong 'WHY' in this industry because it is going to be tough at times - nothing worth achieving is ever going to be easy. On the other hand it is a very worthwhile, rewarding industry to be a part of, but you only get out of it what you put in.

What are the major benefits of the industry?

1) You have no employees. If you've had employees in the past you'll know the pitfalls
2) No requirement for warehousing, shop fronts, industrial units, trucks, vans etc
3) No outlay for stock
4) And in this day and age, the big one – no cash flow problems

Your apprenticeship

If you've grasped the concept and believe in the marketing plan you are ready to start your apprenticeship.
This is the opportunity to work towards the goal where you can choose –

When you want to work
Where you want to work
Who you want to work with

Which all sounds great, I'm sure you will agree.
But most people fail to understand that this is NOT how your business starts,
this is where your business can take you.

It's a journey
It's NOT a 'big bang' event
that signals the birth of your business.

It takes time and learning to get to the privileged position of having choices.
You must be prepared to serve your apprenticeship.

FOR THINGS TO CHANGE YOU NEED TO CHANGE
For things to get better you need to get better
And who can get better?

EVERYONE

In the course of serving your apprenticeship you must learn to take responsibility for your own success. Along the way you will be given lots of help and support, but primarily you will get to where you want to get because of one person - YOU.

<u>Is this really all worth while?</u>

There will be many times, especially in the early days, when you ask yourself – "Is this really all worthwhile? I have put in so much effort which has produced such small financial rewards".

There were many times we called our sponsors with the very same question, and more often than not we did not like their answers!

It was frustrating to be told – "Just focus on the business building activities and don't worry about the results. The results will come if you keep doing the right things". That had to be one of the most frustrating answers when we were frustrated with the current results. But, like us, you will come to understand how that statement is one of the most powerful messages in network marketing.

Study the graph below because it will help you to realise just how worth while it all is. The graph reveals the simplicity of time versus income in this industry. In the early years you put in a great deal of time for little financial return. As the years go by your income rises and you get more and more out of your business for less time spent.

BUT, and it is a very big and important BUT – it won't happen if you don't put in the time and effort in the early years.

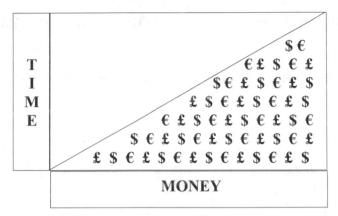

The graph applies as much to part time people as it does to full time distributors. It will underline the message to remember the words of the great Jim Rohn – "Work full time on your job and part time on your fortune, and the day will come when you can work full time on your fortune."

Your monthly cheque is recognition of your efforts. The greater your efforts the greater your recognition. You will have increased your company's turnover and increased your value to your company. Your marketing plan is the stairway to success and the incentives and promotions that are available to everyone.

In the beginning you invest a great deal of time in your business for small financial rewards. But you are building the foundations of a business that will pay you massive rewards in years to come. It is the business that will take you to the privileged position of having choices. This is where network marketing can, and will, take you.

There will be frustrations and disappointments, and times when you think nothing is going right. These are the highs and lows which are the emotional roller coaster of network marketing.

Sometimes the only question is – "Can I hold on?"

Don't give up.

Keep working, for you are still an apprentice in network marketing. Focus on the training you receive for it is such a vital part of the learning process.

Yes, you can hold on. You just need to be tough and patient, and it will all be worth while.

Rewards

Rewards come in many forms in this industry. They can be personal achievement, helping others to achieve, high earning potential, finding your 'WHY' to drive you forward to undreamt levels of accomplishment and satisfaction.

Over the years some of our biggest rewards have been watching our team members achieve their goals. Applauding their success when they reap the financial benefits network marketing has given them. Sharing their excitement when they buy a new car or their dream home, or clear their lives of debt. Sharing their pleasure when they can give their children the things that they were denied.

Despite what it seems, it is no contradiction to say -

"The most wonderful thing about network marketing is working with people.
The most frustrating thing on this planet can be working with people".

BUT

When your team members find their feet
When they are on stage accepting recognition
When your leaders start leading
When your leaders find their independence

Then there will be few times that your job satisfaction is equalled, or that your sense of pride rises to such dizzy heights.

Ye Olde saying:

'When the WHY is big enough'
the
'HOW will appear'

Mistakes and lessons

Mistake no.1
In the early days we believed that the only people who succeeded
were those with inspiration, or those living in desperation.

Lesson no.1
The lesson is that the industry is for everybody.
Find your personal 'WHY',
because that is what really drives you forward.

Mistake no. 2

Worrying is the big mistake.
Worrying about the importance of having a strong WHY.
Worrying about your training programme when everyone, yourself included, is working hard yet the results you expect don't instantly appear.
You can lose focus and your activity can decrease.

Lesson no. 2

Don't expect it all to happen at once.
Keep learning and applying the lessons and the results will follow.
When times are tough keep focused on the business building activities.
Work consistently on your WHY, and you will understand that you and your business are evolving

'Now we will show you how!'

Chapter 3

The System

Before you read this chapter study the diagram entitled 'Proven Success System'. There are five sections which are the five keys to success in network marketing, and we will be examining each one in detail in the following chapters.

The system reflects the strength of an unbroken circle which has no beginning and no end. Each section represents an essential element in the system.

In this chapter we deal with why learning and implementing a proven success system is vital to your business development. Don't skip this chapter, because everyone must understand -

The Power of the System

Every successful business has a system that everyone can follow.

Perhaps the greatest example of this is a household-name international chain of fast food restaurants. Go into one of their restaurants in London, Glasgow, New York, Barcelona, Bangkok or Athens, and order a meal – you will get the same meal in every country.

Have a look at the staff, and what is the average age of the assistants? Probably under twenty years old. So what makes it such a massively successful business? Is it the managers whose average age is about twenty-four? Or is it because they have such a phenomenal system? This is one of the most successful world-wide businesses today, with a billion dollar turnover, yet run at grass-root level by people who (if you are a parent with teenagers, you'll understand!) we can't even get to keep their rooms tidy!

> THAT IS THE POWER OF A SYSTEM

Every successful leader in network marketing has a system. Think of it as part of your job description to learn and become part of that system.
If you want to be a successful leader you must commit to and learn every aspect of the system and become an essential part of it.

Be aware, however, that systems vary from leader to leader and company to company.

Which System Should I Follow?

The one that your successful upline uses.
Why?
Simply, if it is working for him, it will work for you. What you have to do is learn to make it work for you.

Your system must be user-friendly, duplicateable to ensure that everyone can learn and use it; and highlighting its simplicity so that anyone from any background MUST be able to learn and use it.

Avoid the temptation to experiment with other systems, or to try and invent your own. When you have problems or issues your upline will not be able to help you with an unfamiliar system. He or she has already resolved the problems or issues you are facing, crossing those bridges long before you joined the business. They know that their proven system works, how it works and why it works.

We have been with the same company since 1995, using the same tried and tested successful system. We have moved with the times and taken advantage of technology that was not available when we started. For example we used to post out newsletters to our team, then we e-mailed them, now we post them on the team resources website. We prefer to meet prospects face-to-face, answering the questions that concern them most. When we started we used other people's tenth generation photocopied stories, now we have a colour brochure featuring our own team, and an e-brochure for virtual presentations. We also have a DVD to accompany the brochure when sending out information.

The system is core to your success. Other teams or lines may use different systems which more than likely work well. But for you – stick with your successful upline's system.

Beware of Changing Your System

We could write a whole book about people in the industry who changed the system. A prime example was a distributor who built up a successful business and then allowed his ego to take over. He believed he knew better than his upline, and he went in search of the perfect system. He spoke to leaders through-out the entire industry, implementing this idea from one leader and another idea from the next, and introducing changes almost on a fortnightly basis. His hardworking, loyal team became increasingly confused and alienated, and after two years of their leader's indecision had lost all respect for him.

It illustrates how easy it is to lose your way when your ego takes charge and outgrows your ability. How easy it is to ditch the system which was the foundation of your success, and to forget how you achieved your success in the first place. Instead of admitting he had gone off the rails and seeking help to get back on track, this distributor, in his increasing frustration, endangered his team members' businesses and security.

Another distributor committed what can only be described as self-sabotage. His leaders recognised he had the raw energy that could be channelled in the right direction, but there was a lot of work to be done. They worked very closely with him, nurturing his commitment and involvement in the system, until he was on the brink of great success. Then he made the fatal mistake of listening to other people who had no vested interest in him or his future. He took his eye off the simple system that was the foundation of his success. His own leader, and other leaders within the company, urged him to stick to the system that had served him so well. But he listened to his ego, and in due course his business spiralled into decline.

The message is clear. If you are a leader, beware of changing your proven system, of introducing ideas you have not implemented yourself. New ideas must demonstrably work, not just for yourself, but for your team also.

> Moral of the story
>
> IF IT AIN'T BROKE DON'T FIX IT

Be Seen to Be Working the System

On the upside, there are countless stories about those who stick to the system and, by doing so, become hugely successful in network marketing.

To this day we stick unswervingly to the basic daily routines which we committed to at the outset. To earn your team's respect you must be out there, with them in the trenches, implementing the system you advocate, and visibly seen to be doing so. Beware of changing your system, of introducing new ideas you have not fully researched and tested before implementing them yourself. New ideas must be proven to work – not just for yourself, they must work for others too.

Remember we explained in the previous chapter how you can work your way to the privileged position of having choices about when to work, where to work, and with whom you work. We have reached this privileged position now. The single most significant contribution to our good fortune has been our dedication to our proven success system.

'follow a proven success system..'

When you are new to the industry and laying the foundations of your business, be actively involved with your leader and his or her system.

The need for high-profile activity and involvement increases once you are a leader yourself. Openly and enthusiastically working your own system motivates and drives your team (especially the new members) to do the same. Everything must be seen to be duplicateable – that means you need to stay visibly active. We would never ask, train or teach anyone to do anything we haven't ourselves successfully done in the past, or are currently doing.

We refer to 'in the past', because as you advance up the marketing plan, and your team grows, your role will change. For example, in our early days we had to maintain a high level of personal retail – this put food on the table and petrol in the car. It allowed us to attend the vital training evenings and seminars which were designed to educate us to become successful. Now our time is more valuably spent working closely with our new people and future leaders.

Work the System

Go back to the beginning of this chapter and remind yourself about the diagram entitled 'Proven Success System'. Understand that if you ignore any one of the five success points you will restrict the size and potential of the business you have set your sights on. Do not expect to reach the top if you break the success chain.

The powerhouse that drives your business will be the system that has been tested and proven in practice. Never forget, if successful upline leaders are working a system, there must be a reason. They use what they know works for themselves and for others. In Chapter 2 we explained how focusing on the training is such a vital part of your apprenticeship. Working at, and becoming part of, the system is a major part of the learning process of your apprenticeship.

Ye Olde Saying:

'Don't Reinvent the Wheel'

it's round and it works

'Don't Make it Square'

Mistakes and Lessons

Mistake no. 1

Over the years we have seen so many people and their careers fail, by trying to find the perfect system.

Lesson no.1

Work the same proven system that your upline, who is the person after yourself with the most interest in your success, is working.

The system will reflect the growth in your business, evolving and developing with advances in technology. When we started, 'high tech' was a slide presentation and hand-written acetates. Now, 'low tech' is laser-printed acetates and 'high tech' is power point.

Stick with your upline's system to maximise the benefits for your business.

The message is clear –
"If it ain't broke don't fix it".

Mistake no.2

Failing to use all five points of the system. There are no short cuts, and if you do not implement all five sections you won't reach your full financial potential.

Lesson no. 2

It just doesn't work. All five keys to success are required to drive this machine.

If the five main components that move a vehicle forward are the engine, fuel, wheels, steering wheel and the driver – which one do you think you could afford to miss out?

Network Marketing is the same – it is a vehicle that can transform you, and take you to places you never dreamed of.

Let's get this vehicle moving!

Chapter 4

Self Education

People who seek a new career in network marketing rarely have prior experience of the industry. They have skills and experience to contribute to their new business, but few realise at the outset how dependent their future success is on their willingness to become totally teachable. To illustrate the WHY of self-education, or personal development, we need to explain the TAR principle.

The TAR Principle

RESULTS

If you are to benefit fully from the TAR Principle, the first essential is that you must be prepared to confront yourself, and your past performance, with absolute honesty.

Everyone can point to past achievements of a greater or lesser degree. Some may be happy with them, but most of us, if we are honest with ourselves – are not. What attracts most new recruits to network marketing is the belief that they can improve on past performance, and the opportunities for personal success that improved performance presents.

If, after honest self-appraisal, we are not happy with past results – why is that? Generally the answer lies within ourselves, and our past actions. It may seem blunt, but other than serious illness or accident there can be no other reason for poor performance. If you are not happy with past results, it is solely due to your past actions.

As one of our great mentors, Tony Wilson, Chief Executive of Lifestyle Architecture, says: "Many people read books, listen to CD's and even attend seminars, but they forget the MIRACLE part of the whole process – the action part".

ACTION

WHY did we take those past actions
if we are unhappy with the results they produced?

The reason we did so was because of what we were thinking
at the time - there can be no other reason.

If we want better Results in our lives
we must think seriously about taking better Actions.
If we intend to take better actions
we must also start thinking better Thoughts.

People get complacent. They reach a comfort level in their job or business and stop working on themselves and their personal progression as business leaders. If you want things to get better, you need to get better. For things to change, you need to change.

How do we change?

Through continued personal development and application of our new motivation and knowledge.

> The results we currently experience
> are a direct result of past thinking

Our past thinking at any particular time caused us to take our past actions, the consequence of which is our present results.

THINKING + ACTION = RESULTS

A Change In Thinking

As Hazel and I have concentrated on our own personal development we have become more convinced than ever that What you think is What you get. By activating a change in thinking we activate a change in results. Those who have not been introduced to the T + A = R principle are unaware that they can change their results.

When you attend open nights, conferences, training sessions or seminars you are encouraged by the leaders to read books and listen to the training CDs. They know from personal experience the importance of self-education and its contribution to their own success.

Embarking on personal development is a new experience for many people, so listen to the advice about which books to read first. When you have reached higher levels of personal development don't recommend the books you are reading to someone who is in their first year in the industry. Be sure to pitch your recommendations at a level relevant to the individual's experience.

Who can change their thinking?
Anyone who wishes to.

As part of our constant on-going self-appraisal of our business and ourselves we use the table at the end of this chapter. Filling in the columns headed 'What's gone right and WHY?', 'What's gone wrong and WHY?', and 'What needs to change?' helps us focus honestly on the day-to-day viability of our business system.

We were asked to help a distributor who to all appearances was doing the right things, yet his business was declining. How could he pinpoint WHY he was foundering? We asked him to complete our own self-appraisal table and it was immediately obvious where his problems lay.

He had long lists of what had gone right and what had gone wrong, and why in each case. But in the third column – 'need for change' – he had written 'NOTHING' against all the entries. He was not prepared to take personal responsibility for his actions, not prepared to face up honestly to his shortcomings, not prepared to change his thinking. The outcome was that he quit the business shortly afterwards. Fortunately the others in his team were aware of the problem and have gone on to build successful businesses.

Who can change their thinking?
Anyone who wishes to.

If you want success in network marketing you must learn to think like the successful network marketing leaders. Learn to get away from 'getting by' thinking, doing just enough to get by on a day-to-day basis. The results are non-productive and you will just get by on a day-to-day basis!

Average thinking produces 'maintenance' results, reaching a comfort level and maintaining it.

Personal development will move people from 'getting by', or maintenance thinking, to becoming high performers with their thinking focused on progression. High performers' thinking is of abundance and unlimited potential, and drives them to build successful network marketing businesses.

Extract from 'Where does it all START' on Self-Education by John Stephen

'Look at your inventory of life assets. If you made the decision right now, the moment you have read this, that you wanted to live a better life, which life asset would you depend on first to help you achieve this aim?
I would choose the ability to read. For with that single ability, which most of us have, we can perform miracles with our lives. Would you resolve to make a slight change in your daily routine, and when you next have some spare time, instead of

switching on the TV, get yourself some of the wisdom of the world?

Take a trip to your local library or bookshop, visit a company I use, knowledgeisking.co.uk, or amazon.com and introduce yourself to some of the inspirational authors like Napoleon Hill, Jim Rohn, Brian Tracy, Dale Carnegie, Zig Ziglar and John C. Maxwell from whom I have learned so much. They are some of the authors who will help you, just as they helped me, to learn the 'success rules'.

There is a catch of course. My challenge to you may be the first challenge on your road to personal development. If so, then you must go to these mentors as I did, for they will not come to you. When I look back and ask where did my winning attitude come from, I know a lot of it came from self-education.

This is the first book on your road to personal development, but I have no misgivings in encouraging you to widen your ambition horizons by reading and listening to the wisdom of those who have helped me.'

In America they say, "the bigger the house, the bigger the library". How do you think they could afford the bigger house today? Because of yesterday's self-education and personal development!

Ye Olde Saying:

'Great leaders are great readers'

Mistakes and Lessons

Mistake no. 1

When some newcomers join a network and start learning about self-education and personal development, they think they can fast-forward their career if they buy every book available on network marketing, instead of concentrating on reading and listening to material which is relevant to their level of experience in the industry.

Lesson no. 1

You need to read books and listen to CDs when you are new to this industry in order to grasp the basic concepts. But if you squander all your energies reading books and listening to CDs you will have missed the point of self-education, and your progress will reflect this.

Besides learning the basics of the industry you need also to concentrate on your personal development programme. That means developing your business as well as developing your library.

If you are going to be a great leader in this industry you must be able to recommend books and CDs to your team which are relevant to the level of each team member's individual progress up the marketing plan.

Mistake no. 2

Getting to a stage where we feel we've made it; and think we don't need self-education any more.

Lesson no. 2

Self-education keeps us advancing on our journey. It keeps us motivated to consistently climb our chosen marketing plan ladder.

There's a fundamental difference between reading books and learning their lessons – letting them be the building blocks of your personal development plan. We are not talking about novels for entertainment, but treasure chests packed with information and secrets which show you how to become successful.

Reading vs Listening – Years ago John didn't read, although he would listen to every tape or CD available. To this day John prefers to listen and has developed his car into his university. Hazel, on the other hand, is an avid reader, and loses concentration when just listening.

Hazel would read extracts from books to John, who realised that the written word contains more information. He has had to work hard to make the time to sit and read. One of the drivers which motivated him to write his first book, 'Where does it all START', were the struggles he had in the early days of his own personal development with reading. He had also identified a gap in the market for an easy-to-read introduction to starting your personal development programme, especially for people who have never come across the concept.

Get yourself a quality notebook and start taking notes from the books you read and the CDs you listen to. It helps to reinforce the value you have acquired from them, and is useful for future quick reference and to use in your training material. You will be surprised how your outlook will have changed over the years when you review your notes.

| Success Thinking | + | Effective Action | = | Great Results |

What's Gone Right and Why?	What's Gone Wrong and Why?	What needs To Change?

Chapter 5

Work With/Be Teachable

A major principle underpinning Network Marketing, and a major attraction which brings many people into the industry, and retains them, is the knowledge that they can have, and own, their own business. What contributes to your success in this industry is knowing that you are in business for yourself, but not by yourself. You always have your upline to support you.

Unlike conventional business, those who are already established in network marketing are more than willing to pass on their experience and knowledge. They know that your success contributes to their success. Everyone is part of someone else's team. You are part of someone's team, and when you introduce people to this business they become part of your team.

Those who are already established and successful, understand what a serious business this is. They have seen the industry for what it really is, and what it can do for them and their families. They have learnt to work as individuals, following their successful upline's system. But they also understand the power and effectiveness of working together as a team.

Of working for themselves, but not by themselves.

> Even the Lone Ranger had Tonto

Learning to work together and blend as a team takes time, for everyone is different, with differing points of view. It took you time to understand this as you moved up your marketing plan, so understand that it will take your own team time to realise how teamwork generates momentum and continuous excitement within the group.

We now want to introduce you to the best example we know of demonstrating the different types of personalities who join our business. But, first, take a moment to be completely honest with yourself, and identify which area you are currently in.

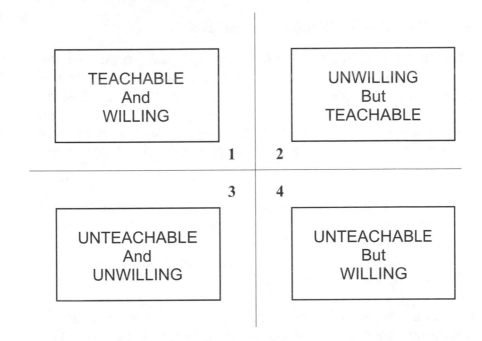

Distributor No.1 Teachable & Willing

This is your dream distributor who commits to the system from the word 'Go'. They communicate regularly with their leaders, go to events without being asked or reminded to do so, move product consistently and are enthusiastic contributors to team building activities. Wouldn't it be great if there were more distributors like this in your team?

Solution: Keep up recruitment activity to maximise your chances of finding more of these people.

Distributor No.2 Unwilling but Teachable

This distributor takes in everything you say, reads all the recommended books, and works through their personal development programme - coming to all the events and taking lots of notes. In reality they do not accept any of the training they are offered, give lip service only to their development programme, and read all the books, but don't apply the learning.

Consequently they do not move products or take steps to start building their own team. Here is someone with the potential to become a serious player in the industry but fails to fulfil their promise. When you are trying to build your successful team, this distributor is extremely frustrating.

Solution: It may take time, but your aim must be to gently encourage them to use a development plan or tracker. You will find an example of the one we use in the Appendix at the end of this chapter. You may wish to rename some of the titles to tailor it to your specific business, but do not change their order of priority. It is the culmination of successful application and has been devised over many years.

Distributor No. 3 Willing but Unteachable

Distributors who have been successful in this or previous occupations can fall into the trap of thinking – "I can do this job. I've been successful before, and I'll do it all my own way". They work on the 'Do it myself' principle, instead of running with their upline's proven techniques.

With their previous skills and experience these distributors have the potential to be dynamic. They can be your future leaders if they are prepared to commit to the system. But they live in the past and want to be independent too quickly. Their downfall is allowing their ego to drive them, and their unwillingness to start again on the bottom rung of the ladder.

Solution: They must step back and accept that they need to use the expertise of their upline and learn the right techniques to build their business. Arrange for them to have a serious one-to-one session with another leader who can give them honest, constructive advice.

Distributor No. 4 Unwilling and Unteachable

We wonder why they signed the application form. Unless they are prepared to radically change, both you and they are heading for a great deal of heartache.

The ONLY solution: Keep them informed when and where events are. If they come they might be inspired. Otherwise they are likely to quit anyway, which will be for the best, as there is no chance of them dragging you down to their level. You can help only those who want to help themselves.

Work With

Within the Network Marketing industry, 'working with' is your ticket to learning, progress and success. It drives on your business plan, helping to grow your business and consequently your income.

When you are new to network marketing, your immediate concern is – "Who will I be working with?" It will likely be your sponsor, or your senior upline, especially if you are starting your new career on a part-time basis. But the great advantage of this business is that there is always someone with a vested interest in your success, who is ready to help and support you.

People who have grasped the basics, who are beginning to feel established in the business, and have achieved a degree of success, sometimes forget that 'Working With' is a key component to their continued growth and advancement. Until you are more successful, earning more money or have progressed further up your marketing plan than any of your upline, you must continue to 'work with' or communicate with people who are far further along the journey you are just starting.

Despite our number of years in this industry we still listen to, and learn from, people more senior to us in our company.

The Principle of 'Working With'

By 'working with' you start to build the process of duplication, which is the basis of this industry's success. Working for yourself, but not by yourself, means you are working your business with someone who is supportive of you, or alternatively who you are supporting – someone who you are passing on your knowledge and experience to. Don't try to 'go it alone'; aim to have a team member with you as often as you can when you go about your daily business.

Working together makes the whole experience more fun. Sharing experiences helps you as well as the people you are 'working with'. Neither you, nor they, can know it all and the newest member of your team has something to pass on and share with the most senior member. Car journeys between appointments are ideal opportunities to bounce ideas back and forth, and discuss individual business problems and answer questions.

Your aim is to build the power of duplication into your business. In practical terms this means communicating your system to each new team member. They in turn must show you they have learned enough to work their business and are capable of showing it to others. The only way this can happen is by all team members 'working with' and communicating with each other.

Who Do I 'Work With'

'Working with' works in two directions. It's not just who you work with for your own advancement. If you want to be a successful leader you must develop the ability to recognise who to work with in your team. Developing the ability to recognise your future leaders is essential.

A common mistake is automatically identifying your frontline people as your future leaders; in effect wanting more success for them than they may want for themselves. You need to look at your team as a whole and 'dig for gold' at all levels. Hopefully your frontline people will be your future leaders, but as your business grows the 'cream rises'.

Several years ago one of our team was showing promise and successfully developing up the marketing plan. Sadly he was distracted by personal problems and eventually quit the business. In his emotional state he failed to recognise that in the course of all the good work he had done, he had been developing a potential leader. That leader has gone on to become one of our company's most dynamic producers, with a business which turns over £millions.

Uncertainty can arise when you, as leader, recognise the potential in someone to be a big player, and they do not readily fall into the 'Teachable and Willing' box. Be patient and let that person develop enough to see for themselves that they can, and will, be a big player. Whatever you do – Don't let that person go! Keep in touch, keep the lines of communication open, encourage and advise them until they are ready.

Who will be my leaders?

Here is the answer we got to that self-same question from one of our senior successful upline –

> "If you can learn to live with the fact:
> That what you know, is you don't know
> You will earn a fortune"

Not the answer we were looking for at the time. He went on to explain: "You don't know who will, and who won't join your business. You don't know who will and who won't build a team. The only thing you know is, you don't know".

Contradictory as it sounds, it was wise advice. We don't know who will join us and who won't, so we need to show and tell everybody about the benefits of working in our wonderful network marketing industry.

We actively continue to build our own business and are constantly reminded of the impact of the statement. If like us, you understand and accept that you don't know who will join you, or who will become your leaders; and, if like us, you have the passion and drive to tell everyone about our wonderful networking industry –

YOU WILL EARN A FORTUNE

Ye Olde saying:

'The only thing you know is you don't know'

Mistakes and Lessons

Mistake no. 1
Working with the wrong people.

Lesson no. 1
We have worked with people in the past, who were the right people.
But changes in their personal circumstances have changed them, so that they were no longer the right people.
Keep focused on your master plan, work with the Teachable and Willing people who are in box number 1, and develop solutions to help and support others to get into that box.

Mistake no.2

Forgetting that until you are more successful, earning more money or at a higher position in your marketing plan than any of your upline, you still need to 'work with', and take advice from time to time, in order to reach the highest levels.

Lesson no. 2

Continually work with your successful upline. Be wise enough to take advice from the right people. You may not agree with or like the answers you are given, but if you want to succeed, consult continually and take action on the advice.

BUSINESS DEVELOPMENT PLAN FOR: NAME

EMAIL: Tele No:

WEEK COMMENCING:…………

ACTIVITY	FRI	SAT	SUNDAY	MON	TUES	WEDNES	THURS	TOTALS
CALLS MADE FROM LISTS								
FLYERS OUT								
ADS PLACED SHOP CARDS								
INFO PACKS SENT								
TOTAL RESPONSES								
PRESENTATIONS								
FOLLOW UP CALLS								
EVENT ATTENDED								
TEAM SIZZLE								
THE BOOK I'M STUDYING								
NO. SIGNED INTO GROUP								
NO. IN PIPELINE								
PRODUCT or SERVICE MOVED								

TOTAL ORDERS FOR WEEK= £

TOTAL NO OF ACTIVE PEOPLE IN TEAM THIS WEEK =

HOW DO YOU FEEL
ABOUT YOUR PROGRESS

Any lessons Learned?

Chapter 6

Retail Product or Service

'Retail Products'

For any networking company to be successful, products or services must be moved to an end user.

Every company differs on product ranges, marketing plan and qualification levels for bonuses and commissions. Some companies add incentives, special promotions and cash bonuses. Find out from your successful upline what you personally have to do to qualify for benefits, and target them.

Because of the method of marketing in networking, retail profit is usually fairly high. Cutting out all the 'middle men' and conventional overheads of warehousing, premises, distribution costs, marketing costs and the like, means your company can pass on the benefits to you, the distributor.

The savings are paid out in the form of high initial commission and bonuses.

Personal Retail Plan

How much product or the level of services you need to personally retail is usually based on 'leading by example'. We ourselves don't expect or ask anybody to do anything we don't currently do ourselves, or have done in the past, whether it is business building or retailing product.

Be realistic when working out retail plans for yourself and your team. A person working part-time in the business will not have the same time available as someone full-time. But everyone needs a personal retail plan which will consistently move products to the end users. The secret to consistently moving product is being consistent with your weekly or monthly plan.

If your company has a very wide product range some people will join it solely to move products. For the right people it is quite possible to earn a substantial income by consistently moving high volumes of products. If you have joined such a company, and wish to become a high volume retailer, seek out those in your company who are already doing so and ask their advice and help.

People who join only to retail products can broaden their activities to include business building. Encourage these people to come to events where they can get advice from other successful retailers. Hopefully they will see the bigger picture and attend more and more events, and gain the experience to make the move into business building if they choose to, or if their circumstances change.

Believe in Your Product

Some network marketing companies have specialist products which need to be demonstrated or explained to potential customers. Work with your experienced upline to learn how to do this.

Whatever your company's product range you should become as familiar with as much of it as you can. How many of the products you personally use will depend on the size of the range. The bigger the range the more you will use. If you cannot endorse your own company's products from personal experience, how can you expect others to buy them?

The company we represent has an enormous product range. When we joined it we didn't empty the house and replace everything immediately; we couldn't afford to. But as items needed replacing we did so from our own company's range.

If you want to build a successful business you need to develop belief in the products you move to the end user. If you don't have that belief you are unlikely to build a successful business.

> Customers can become Distributors

Everyone should aim to build up their customer base because customer loyalty is what you are aiming for. If you look after your customers you are more likely to get repeat business. Your customers need to know how to get hold of you, so give them your business card or put labels with your contact details on the products they have bought from you. Make it easy for them; you don't know where they could lead you. They may simply wish to replace or purchase more products for themselves or they may refer their friends to you as potential customers.

More importantly, customers can become distributors, so make sure they have your telephone number and e-mail address at the very least.

The core concept, generally, of network marketing is of a lot of people each doing a little to cumulatively produce a lot. (Although some companies' marketing methods do allow substantial income to be derived solely from retailing products). One of the best leaders in our own business had one of the worst starts with his retail activities. In his first month he would have earned all of £21 from his personal efforts. Because he had grasped the concept and had started team building straight away, he actually earned £100 per week in his first month and now turns over £millions.

Party Plan

Some companies who use Party Plan as their method of marketing are also networking companies. If you are involved with such a company you will be given training in how use their system, along with brochures, company invitations and a demonstration pack.

Depending on your product range you may also wish to consider Party Plan as an optional method to retail products. Even if your company doesn't supply a demonstration kit or pack, you can create your own. It can be a very successful method of retail and good fun to do.

Party Plan is not just for girls; men are more than capable of demonstrating the products. People usually think only of house parties when they think of Party Plan, but there are endless other suggestions to get in front of people. Local clubs and associations are always looking for ways to raise funds. Old folks homes, schools, the local pub are all excellent venues to move your products, so don't dismiss Party Plan.

Ye Olde Saying:

'Retail is the backbone of the business'

Mistakes and Lessons

Mistake no. 1
Thinking –"What if nobody buys anything from me?"

Lesson no. 1
Your company wouldn't exist if its products or services couldn't move to an end user. The whole concept of network market-ing is whether you want to earn 100% of your own efforts, or 1% of 100 others? A successful company in the network marketing business does not rely on you alone. Your task is to find your customers, make your retail plan, and stick with it. If it works for others it can work for you, but you need to apply consistency and persistency to achieve a result.

Mistake no. 2
Looking for people who only want to retail product.

Lesson no.2
High retailers, especially, make this common mistake. They want to build a retail business because they believe in the products' ability to move to the end user – they've proved that themselves. It's also a common mistake for new people who haven't fully grasped the concept of how a network company works. They actively show their business as either a retail based business or a retail opportunity only, instead of showing how powerful the concept of network marketing really is. Our philosophy was, and still is, that we are always looking for team leaders, and on the way we will find some good people who focus only on retailing product.

Some people miss the true meaning of 'Retail is the back-bone of this business'. We started this chapter by saying that your product or services MUST reach an end user. If no one moves any product or service you won't have a business and your company will not exist. Perhaps 'Ye Olde Saying' should read – 'Product and services moving to an end user are the backbone of this business'.

Chapter 7

Introduce Others

People make a great mistake thinking that 'no one I know will be interested in getting involved in network marketing', and it's an outlook that can really slow down your business development. In this chapter we take you through several proven methods to help you introduce others to your business.

Essentially, success in network marketing depends on two things – your success at playing the numbers game, and how successfully you follow the system your upline advocates. Remember your upline is there to help you become successful. His or her own success depends on it.

We always come back to the old networking story which, for us, gets the point across on how to build your business fast.

magine the scenario – You are driving along a country road and you have a puncture. While you are fixing it you see something shining in the bushes at the roadside. You go to investigate, and to your delight discover it is a bar of gold. In your excitement you hunt through the bushes to see if there are any more. You come across a cave, and when you look inside it is filled with more gold bars. There are far too many for you to carry away on your own, so what should you do?

Would you rush home, phone the local newspaper and place an advert saying 'Help wanted FREE gold bars'. Or would you phone your family and friends to tell them about your amazing discovery. Do you get the point?

Discovering networking is the same. It's a gold mine. It's the best kept secret that you want to share with everybody. So your family and friends should be the first people you let into the secret.

Even if they don't have an immediate interest,
the important thing is
they know what you are doing.

And they may know someone who is interested.

The List

We built our business on contact lists because we couldn't afford to advertise or pay for flyers and business cards, and the Internet was in its very early days too. At the start, all we could afford to do was telephone everyone we knew and ask if we could show them our new business idea.

We were given an exercise to help us put together our first prospect list to start us off. Imagine, for the purpose of the exercise, that network marketing and your business don't exist. You are simply compiling a list of categories of people you know. The list is not a 'one-off' exercise, it's a work-in-progress exercise, and you will be continually adding to your list. Take your time doing the exercise; we use it regularly in training sessions and it works very well.

On an A4 sheet of paper line out five sections. The aim is to have five different names in each section. Don't be like the new distributor who wrote the same names in each section! You want a lot more names than that. At this stage don't think about what you may have to say to all these people; don't think which of them will or will not join your business, because for the time being network marketing and your business don't exist.

Category 1: Write down the names of five people who you know could use an extra £100, $100 or €100 a week, right now.

That wasn't too difficult, was it?

Category 2: Next, five people you know who wouldn't be greatly interested in an extra £100 etc. per week, but would definitely be interested in an extra £1000 etc. per month.
Many people who have done this exercise have said that everyone they know has got a good job with a good income. Our research of people with good jobs and high incomes has shown that many people earning £30000 a year are spending £31000. Why is this? Because in these days of credit cards, remortgaging and the like, the market place allows it and even encourages it.

So you can help someone whose income has peaked at £30000, to earn an extra £12000 per annum. Imagine the impact and benefit that can have on that person's lifestyle. It could mean a new house, a new car, help them to pay off debt, it might save a mortgage (and save the family home), and it might even save a marriage.

Category 3:   Now, five people you know who have a mortgage.

Category 4:   Five people you know who have a car.

Category 5:   This is an easy one! Five people whose names you haven't already written down.

You can substantially increase the numbers in your list with the names of all the people in your mobile phone or e-mail address book. Then there's all those on your Christmas card list. If you were going to have the biggest party ever, who would be on the invitation list? Who would you invite to the wedding if one of your children got married?

The number of names on your list is probably running into several hundreds already. If ten new people joined your team and those ten new people all did this same exercise, the lists would number thousands. So it is easy to see how your prospect list is always going to be a work-in-progress list as you add to it at every chance you get.

```
┌─────────────────────────────────────────┐
│                 WARNING                  │
│           Never prejudge people.         │
│    What you do know is you don't know    │
│                                          │
│          You don't know who will         │
│      And who won't join your business    │
└─────────────────────────────────────────┘
```

Our job is simply to show prospects our business to the best of our ability. People join this industry for all sorts of reasons, but most of them do so because the timing is right for them.

While the time to join your team may be just right for some of the people on your list, what we know that we don't know is whether your business is right for them or not. So you will understand how important your presentation, its message and its impact are to the growth and success of your business.

There's one thing for sure, if your family and friends don't know about your business, if the people on your prospect list don't see and hear your presentation, they will never join YOU. People in our team have appeared with guests who are friends or relations of other team members who hadn't thought to bring them along as guests themselves because they thought they would not be interested!

ANOTHER THING WE KNOW THAT WE DON'T KNOW is whether someone who joins our team will be good. It's every individual's own decision how successful they become. Your key people and your future leaders will soon show you who they are by becoming part of the system, working it and contributing to it.

Confident new people will tell you how massively successful they intend to be. But remember – the only thing you know is that you don't know. Actions talk louder than words, and in their early days these big talkers may be less successful than they boasted. But if they are trying hard you and your upline can show them how to find their level of productive effectiveness, and help them to improve their ratios.

Advertising

Advertising can be very effective, but it can be expensive too. New people often place adverts that you know are not effective and simply waste their money. Consult with the people in your upline who run effective advertising campaigns and can advise you on effective wording. Be teachable, use the wording for advertisements that has been proven to work.

We have noticed that if someone joins our team from an advertisement, that is how they will want to build their own business. Advertising works, but it is not the only method. Learn to use all the methods promoted by your company. The larger the net you spread the more prospects you will attract.

Flyers and Business Cards

Again it is important to use effective and persuasive language. This method relies heavily on the numbers game and you have to distribute enough of each to make the phone ring or provoke an e-mail response. It is a good way to create leads but you must be persistent and consistent. Use the tracker/ business development plan to check your success and identify how many flyers and/or cards are needed to generate a reasonable response. The image needs to match the opportunity you are promoting.

The Internet

Make best use of technology. Put up your own website and attract direct hits to it. Visit a site many of our team use www.thewebcrew.com. You will find more information there and exciting offers specifically designed for network marketing. There is also an informative article giving advice on making best use of your web site for networking.

As more and more people use the Internet daily this can help generate a lot of interest in your business. Always include your web site address on all cards, flyers and advertisements.

As ever, take advice from your upline on the wording for your web site. There are probably company guidelines or specific rules that must be adhered to. Be aware that the rules of copyright also apply to the Internet. If you want to use stories or images of other people you must ask their permission first. Take good advice, and don't waste money on creating a site that may not work or may be illegal.

Success in network marketing comes from consistently playing the numbers game. It's all about lead generation. The more leads you can produce by all the methods available, and the more leads you chase, the greater the chance you give yourself of getting people in your team. So that you really understand the power of numbers we will expand on playing the numbers game in another chapter.

Mistakes and Lessons

Mistake no. 1
Cutting back or stopping lead generation and prospecting activities altogether because the first five or ten contacts were unsuccessful.

Lesson no. 1
Focus on the activity and the results will follow. Keep working closely with your upline, the more you practise the better you get. How do you know that the next contact will not be your major player? Building your team is truly a numbers game. Understand it, accept it and get on with it.

Mistake no.2
Focusing on too few methods of lead generation and ignoring the importance of having a prospect list.

Lesson no. 2
Remember that your prospect list is a work-in-progress list. We still work on, and augment, our own list to this day. Maximise the potential of working your list. Start with –

Who You Know

progress with

Who They Know

and advance with

Who You Meet

69

Chapter 8

Build For Events

"Building for Events"

Many years ago when our business was still small, we were told that if we wanted to earn really 'serious' money, to become so rich that when we climbed into our brand new, bright red Ferrari we couldn't close the door for the £50 notes falling out of it - we had to learn to build for events. An amusing story, but the underlying message contains a great deal of truth.

> 'If you can learn how to build for events you
> will become wealthy'.

The more people you can encourage to come to events, the larger your team will grow. It sounds simple, and it is.

We regularly see distributors make the same mistake time and time again. Distributors who don't come to events are missing out. They are missing the buzz that events create. The 'stay-at-homes' will probably do as little today as they did yesterday, or maybe even less!

But if they attend events there is every chance they will be inspired, educated and motivated - which means that tomorrow they will want to do a bit more. They will be motivated at least until the next event. Consistent attendance at events means consistently being motivated.

> Events are the glue that holds the team
> and the system together.

Only by attending events will you learn the system. Events are life-changing catalysts; they give you and your team the wings to fly. We can recognise, as does your own successful upline, from those who attend events, who we should work with and who will be the team leaders of tomorrow. You identify your future leaders from those who you see regularly at events, for those key people reveal themselves by working the system. If you want your business to grow you must learn to use and to build for events.

Attend all the events you can; you don't know which ones will inspire you or your team.Note that the system says 'EventS', not an event!

Events

Most established network marketing companies have events, mostly organised by the successful distributors within that company. All events have a specific purpose – education, recruitment, motivation, inspiration and all events should include a recognition spot   acknowledging distributors' successes.

> Leaders can be found at ALL the events.

Open nights – Some refer to these as 'opportunity meetings'.

As we built up our team we realised that for many people who spend much of their working day attending meetings, the thought of yet another 'meeting' in the evening was quite off-putting. Likewise, the word 'meeting' was obviously intimidating for people coming to the introductory presentation for the first time who did not work in an office environment.

So we changed the title to 'Open Nights', which is altogether more user-friendly, with a much more relaxed and informal impact.

Open Nights are for prospects who are "just looking", and those starting out on their new career; and they are definitely for all current distributors. The aim of open nights is to invite new people to meet the established distributors, to hear the business opportunity presentation, and experience the buzz of the recognition spot.

The more people you invite to your Open Nights the faster your business will grow. We hold them monthly on a week night, which allows new prospects to come for an overview without interfering with their daytime commitments. We usually include a brief training slot.

A New Format – Our leaders changed the format of our local open nights. The new format is very welcoming, social and friendly and has proved successful and popular with existing distributors. We start with coffee which allows the new people to meet and talk to the leaders. This is followed by a couple of short, light training slots which aim to get new people started, distributors motivated and then drive everyone on to the next big event.

> The most exciting open night you will ever attend is the one you have most guests at!

Basic Training – At these events you learn and teach the day-to-day basics of running your own business and the principles of team building. In our experience 98% of attendees are already involved with the network in question. The other 2% are close to joining and have come along to learn about the next stage, and see what their day-to-day commitment will be. Reinforce training by using all parts of the system as guidelines and subject matter.

The training material used can either be in a set format such as from a manual, or may be your own individual presentation. The events are larger, and usually more informal than open nights, and in the course of training practical advice and useful tips are exchanged.

Workshops – or Seminars. These are generally larger than the basic training and open nights. They are more motivational and can include guest speakers. This is where you will see the bigger picture and meet some of the top distributors.

Leadership Development – These events are for people who want to progress their business - the future leaders and key people within your team. Here, more in depth training is offered to the serious players to help them develop advanced skills and knowledge. Training in your company's systems and procedures takes place. Also, communication skills and the leadership principles required to build a large network are taught.

Depending on the size of your team these events may start off as small in-house groups. They are more relaxed and for smaller groups.

Own Group Sizzles – Any location which is relaxed and fun is good for these events. If you have sizzle sessions in your home you may wish to provide coffee and sandwiches, or even a bottle of wine. Always dispose of the business of the day first, and then new people in the group can be encouraged to ask questions.
Sizzles can incorporate conference calling, and having leaders from other lines, groups or areas sharing their knowledge and experience.

Company Events – Regional, national or international, these are the events where you will definitely see 'The Big Picture'. At these events you hear from top network leaders and company personnel. New products, new incentives and promotions are announced at these events. Everyone is buzzed up and the excitement from such large events has to be experienced. What ever you do, never miss a company showcase.

Recognition

Recognition of success and achievement, in whatever form, is very important at every event. Our experience is that people will often do more for recognition than anything else.

Most people are hard working and do a good job, but never receive so much as a 'thank you' at the end of a job well done. This is where we, in network marketing, can be different and recognise people for their efforts and make them feel appreciated.

Having recognition shows that the system and the business works for new and existing distributors alike. We have a large team and nothing is more rewarding, and gives us a greater sense of pride, than seeing lots of our people cross the stage to receive the recognition they deserve.

People who are being recognised and rewarded are progressing up the marketing plan, earning more money each step they take.

> If you are having a good week,
> the meeting needs you.
> If you are having a bad week,
> you need the meeting.

Conference calling - Until recently this was only available via telephone with a loud-speaker. Now conference calling via the Internet is available.

Video conferencing – As more and more people get Internet connections and with broadband users increasing daily, video calling events will become more and more commonplace. Embrace technology and keep moving with the times.

Other events - Includes working with your upline 1-on-1 whether it is on a business presentation or as a personal consultation. Your upline has given up his or her time to help you, so appreciate it and make the event worthwhile.

Fun - Socialising with your team creates close bonds, and partners and families have an opportunity to meet leaders and other team members. Great friendships have been formed from some of the social events we have organised.
Fun ideas include a night out bowling, a summer BBQ for all the family, a Christmas Dinner and Dance, a day out at the park with games for all the family, corporate go-karting, paint ball. Be creative: all these things are great for team spirit. If a team member has an uncooperative spouse a social day is a great way of letting them meet leaders and colleagues, so that they realise it's not a cult their partner has joined!
Events can be large or small. It doesn't matter, they create synergy.

Maximise All Events

Have the dates and details of all events in your diary. Always take a team member, or a prospect if appropriate, with you – it's one of the things that helps your business to grow.
If you don't attend events how do you expect your team to attend? Leading by example will duplicate this essential part of the system into your business.

Offer to pick up prospects or other guests who you have invited to one of your open nights. 100% of people picked up for a night out attend the party!

If all successful leaders attend events that's a massive clue to success. If all the big earners are at the events it tells us we need to be there too. At the events you associate with the right people.

In an e-mail to the great Jim Rohn, we told him about our activities and plans for the future. In his reply, Jim spoke about the power of association, of being in the right environment and mixing with like-minded people. Of associating with people who are where you want to be.

Ye Olde saying:

'Not everyone who attends the events is successful'

but

'Everyone who is successful attends the events'

Mistakes and Lessons

Mistake no 1
Going to only to a few events, or worse – only one!

Lesson no 1
Events are your office. If you only went to your office once or twice you wouldn't have a job for very long.

Mistake no 2
Attending events, listening to every word, but not taking notes.

Lesson no 2
Have a notebook with you at all events and take notes. Notes help you remember what each speaker was teaching, and you can review at a later date. Many distributors take great notes but omit the reviewing part – this is when you can think about what was said, and how you can apply it to your business.
Learn from the speakers and presenters. Take every opportunity to learn how the business works. Be hungry for the knowledge that will make you successful.

Chapter 9

Communication

"Communication"

Work hard on your communication skills. It will help in every area of your business from telephone conversations to business meetings, from formal presentations to informal team activities, from 1-on-1 meetings with your new people to helping and supporting your team.

The whole essence of communication binds networking together because we don't have offices or a daily workplace to meet with colleagues. It can be lonely working from home, especially when you are used to having somewhere to go every day with a purpose.

Communication is ALWAYS a two-way affair and the networking industry is a people business. It is by working on your communication skills that you will build relationships with people.

BABY SITTING

When people are new to the industry your ability to communicate will be a major factor in ensuring that they get off to a fast start and stay with the programme. We call this baby-sitting. It can be a fine balance how often you phone them or otherwise keep in touch.

Someone new is a baby in the business. Once they become more established and reach a level of success, it's like moving into their teenage years. Like teenagers they may rebel and try to do things their own way. As their leader you must maintain regular communication, passing on information until they mature into adults who have gained the knowledge, experience and understanding of how the industry and business works.

If you build strong relationships with your team members in their early days, you will be able to ride the waves through their teenage years until they mature into the business.

> IT'S NOT WHAT YOU SAY,
> IT'S THE WAY THAT YOU SAY IT

Be careful what you say and how you say it. Don't be like the would-be leader who phoned his team members and demanded answers, instead of remembering that the purpose of his call was to see how they were getting on, and offer help and support. As your team are all self-employed they do not have a boss or a manager. Your role as sponsor is to ensure that you help, support and advise.

In their early days your new people need you to be contactable. When they are having a crisis it's a major crisis to them, and they need you to be available. If you are uncontactable for your team when they need you, they will soon lose respect and trust for you. You are running a business, so an answering machine on your landline or subscribing to an answering service is essential, and your mobile phone keeps you in touch while on the road.

In this chapter we deal with some of the essential tools which will aid communication in your business. We don't require our team members to use every tool that may be available to them; some people like to read messages and others prefer to listen to them. But use as many tools as possible to pass on and share positive information and to receive it yourself.

Your relationship with your upline and your team's relationship with you are built on regular, clear communication. It's how you know how your team are feeling. It brings both positives and negatives out for open discussion, and helps nurse your new people over the first hurdles in their new career. One of the easiest ways to spot if any of your team members are feeling low, or even thinking of quitting, is through their lack of communication.

THE TOOLS OF COMMUNICATION

Telephone

Voice Mail: Voice mail allows you to leave a message on your recipient's personal phone. Think about the message you want to leave and what you want to say before you dial. Messages should be short, positive and relevant. Speak clearly and slowly. Unlike email, voice messaging lets you express emotion. And the system allows you to communicate to your whole team with one phone message.

You can also include your mail box number in your advertisements. This is an excellent second telephone number that lets you keep your home number private. It enhances your business professionalism by not having children answer business calls, and ensures that family members do not delete important messages.

This system also allows you to choose a dialling code which does not restrict your number to one area. A widely used company www.mlmmessaging.com gives the option of a free telephone number in another country, accessed from your home telephone.

Personal live telephone calls: Never let technology interfere with basic, personal human contact. You can leave messages, send emails, send text messages but nothing is more appreciated than a personal phone call.

Conference Calling: Can be used as part of a team sizzle session, a live training event, and individuals can join in direct from home or office.

Text Messaging: Text messages can be sent by mobile/cell phone to a landline telephone or computer, not just another mobile phone. The latest computer programmes also permit text messages to be sent to mobile phones.

Some people like to read messages
Some prefer to listen to them

Use as many tools as possible to pass on and share positive information, and to receive it yourself.

Computer

We believe that emails are only for passing on information and for dealing with problems immediately. You cannot put emotion and empathy into an email. Computers are now an entrenched part of daily business life and we see people choosing email as their main channel of communication. Be aware, however, that email has a different impact from a personal telephone call and can be misread and misunderstood.

Email – For sending and receiving messages and passing on news. We have a saying - 'better to receive twice than not at all'. As the only thing we know is that we don't know, pass on all information to your team. You, personally, may not find certain information useful, but some of your team will, although you may not know it at the time. Keep emails short and to the point; people don't like long-winded messages.

Ecards – Recognition is a vital part of the network marketing industry. Receiving an ecard in recognition of success can mean a lot, especially to a new person.

Email loop – We call our team email loop 'hotnews', because we have we embraced the technology which helps us pass on information. We don't use the loop for training purposes, but we use it to notify our team of company and team news. Keep messages short and to the point.

Internet – Blogs require the recipient to visit the blog page in order to keep up-to-date, but not everyone has the necessary high level of interest to do this. Hence the email loop will ensure that all team members receive important information messages. Some on-line companies provide free instant messaging systems which can be used at pre-arranged times to have an online sizzle.

Team Resources web site – The leader of a large team should be utilising this tool to distribute all useful files and links relevant to the business. We also use our team resources web site to post team newsletters. Updates and changes to team resources are notified via the email loop. For smaller teams blogs may also be used as an alternative.

Web Cam – Especially effective for long distance conferencing because it puts a face behind the voice. Use for personal conversations or team sizzles.

Video Conferencing – Gives live training online or through a television screen. If these are streamed on a web site it is possible to access the system at a time that suits the individual.

Web Sites – These provide information only. Enlist the services of a professional to ensure your website looks the part and promotes a professional business image.
The key to a successful website is to keep the text punchy and informative.
Use your website to its full potential. If you have a submission form keep a data base of everyone who replies. Timing may not be right for some people right now, but if you have their contact records you can re-contact them at a later date.

'You are only one click away' from capturing your viewer or losing him or her. If you load your website with graphics that take time to download or appear on screen, your visitor is gone in one click. A company specialising in network marketing web site design is www.thewebcrew.com

As a general rule be very careful about purchasing email addresses. If lists have not been genuinely subscribed to, or the 'names' have not consented to their email address being published, your emails can be reported as spam and your email address suspended.

The Post

The services provided by the postal authorities are still very relevant.

Information Packs – As the name suggests the prospect packs you send out are to provide information. A follow-up phone call will maximise their value and increase their success rate.

Cards – Send congratulation cards to recognise success. Christmas cards are an opportunity to send season's greetings and include your up-to-date business news to family, friends and personal contacts. Remember - timing is important in people's lives.

Mailing Lists – How well qualified the names on such lists are, cannot be guaranteed. They can be over 2 years old and being sold to more than one person. Investigate the currency and quality of all lists before you buy.
Keep accurate records of prospects you have sourced yourself and re-contact them periodically.

Mistakes and Lessons

Mistake no. 1
When someone is new to the industry, excited about having their own business without a boss, they don't see the need to communicate upline.

Lesson no. 1
The early days are the vital time to establish your two-way communication procedures. Only by communicating are you able to ensure everyone is on track, doing the right tasks and heading for success. Communication is needed to embed a new person into your proven success system. The newest people in your team need most help and support, so work on your baby-sitting skills.

Mistake no. 2
Some established people, who have started to build their own team, consistently rely on their upline to communicate and pass on information to themselves and their team members.

Lesson no. 2
If you wish to be recognised as a notable leader you need to learn through the system that you MUST take responsibility for your own success and the success of your team. Take steps to establish your independence by asking for the knowledge and information for yourself from your successful upline, and then duplicate it by communicating it to everyone in your own team.

Chapter 10

Timing & Planning

'Timing and Planning'

Network Marketing offers high rewards to those who follow the system. Everyone who joins the industry wants to earn a high income and create a quality lifestyle for themselves and their families, straight away. But if Rome wasn't built in a day, nor should you expect your network marketing business to be either.

Structure

It takes time to put your business structure in place and build a strong, sound business that will eventually pay you a residual income. For the purposes of this book, however, we believe we are not in a position to advise on structure unless you are in the same company as us and working the same system. Structure can be a very complex thing. Your successful upline knows how your business should be best structured for you, to maximise your income and your security based on your company's marketing plan.

We recall phoning our upline in the early days to complain that despite the enormous effort we were putting into our business, we were not receiving adequate financial return. It hadn't taken us long to start earning a good income and we felt our efforts deserved more.

Our upline assured us we were carrying out the right activities, and our ratios were good and improving. We were definitely on the right tracks, and he advised us - 'Keep doing what you are doing and the financial rewards will catch you up, and one day they will pass you by'. It clearly demonstrated the validity of the time/money graph which we explain in the chapter entitled "WHY?"

We were working hard at our business, and on our personal growth and understanding of the business and the industry. But patience has never been one of John's strong points. However, despite our efforts and our unquestionable service to our deserving team members, we were being unrealistic.

It didn't take us long to realise that the big benefits that we expected to enjoy in the later years of our business could only become reality if we put in the hours and effort in the early years. We could only enjoy the fruits of our hard work if we maintained our level of endeavour and carried on with the correct activities.

ALLOW TIME TO IMPROVE YOUR RATIOS

Phone calls, presentations, adverts, flyers and internet activity are just some of the tools you employ to increase productivity, as you strive to become more effective as quickly as possible, and build a successful business. But you must allow your business enough time to develop so as to be able to measure the success of your activities.

Every business needs a plan and
this business is no different.

The Business Plan

It is not uncommon for new people to be disappointed with the initial production ratios which they achieve from their initial activities. Once you understand your ratios you learn to become more effective. It can only be achieved if you keep accurate records of your activities using trackers or other proven recording methods. Keeping accurate records will allow for accurate measurement when discussing with your upline how you can improve your results.

> What Gets Measured Gets Done

You must have a business plan, but the key is having a plan with flexibility built into it. In our business you cannot work to a strict, rigid plan; you must build discretion and flexibility into it.

Start with an outline plan, a framework to build your flexible plan around. It's a great bonus when your plan works well, but always be ready to respond to sudden change and apply the flexibility your plan permits.

Often you just never know where results are going to show. There have been occasions when we have been working to a particular end, and our endeavours have produced positive results from an entirely different direction.

You may be convinced you are working with the right people, people who are showing great promise, then BOOM – they have left you and their career, for reasons only they understand! That is how networking goes.

We don't think you ever get used to these situations, but it's the nature of our industry. People come and people go, and we'll never be able to change that.

We don't have the normal corporate headaches: we have people instead.

The wonderful thing about network marketing is
we work with people,
and the most frustrating thing you can do in your life is
work with people.

Your Personal Activity Plan

This is your personal plan for retail, lead generation and business building activity. Sit down with your upline and work backwards from your WHY to ascertain the daily and weekly activities required to achieve it.

Your personal activity plan is different from your business plan. You are in control of your own activities and can therefore stick strictly to your personal activity plan. You are not in control of your team's activities so your business plan must have the flexibility to deal with the unexpected when it occurs.

One Step at a Time

If you want to reach the top pin levels, if you want to be the one on stage getting recognition for earning the big cheques, you need a plan that will take you there.

1st 90 days Plan

This is your first plan, an action plan which spotlights your activities and goals for your first exciting ninety days in the marvellous network marketing industry.

In 90 days, where do I want to be?
What do I want to have achieved?

The first 90 days are the crucial time in any new business. It's when new people can be at their most vulnerable, and when most baby-sitting needs to be done. Remember, this is a business and businesses take time, and you need the discipline to stick with it.

It's about focusing on your WHY while concentrating your activity in the NOW. Making each minute, each hour, and each day count using the TNT principle of 'Today Not Tomorrow'

> Focus on the future – your WHY
> BUT concentrate in the NOW

When you can sit down in your chair at the end of the day, and say, "Yes, today I deserve my WHY". When you have completed all your activities for the day, and really worked the business, and you just know you deserve your WHY, there's hardly a feeling in the world to beat it.

You've had a good day. Imagine what would happen if you could do this for a week – what kind of week would you have? You would get your business momentum rolling. If you did this for a month, it is fair to say you would have had a good month. Do this for 90 days and you are settled into a routine. A routine that will embed the momentum into your business that's needed to take you to your WHY. Do this for a year and it will be a great year.

A wonderful thing about network marketing is you can re-start your 90-day plan at any time. Years down the line you can boost your business with a 90-day action plan.

PLANS SAVE TIME

In our industry it's easy to waste time, especially when you are engaged in it full-time. Don't fall into the trap of thinking - 'I've got all day, and if I don't do it today I've got all day tomorrow'. This is fatal thinking and it is easier than you may imagine to get into an undisciplined downward routine, especially if you have never been self-employed before.

The best form of time management we know is to make a 'To Do' list. Every day make a 'To Do' list for the following day. Your list must have at least ten tasks on it. Number them in order of importance, start at number one and do not finish until your list has been completed.

The Perfect Plan

Some people believe that the perfect plan exists, and they spend time and waste energy trying to create it. Sitting at the kitchen table or your office desk drawing circles, filling boxes, investigating every possibility, is wasted effort – the perfect plan doesn't exist. So instead of wasting more time, focus your activities and plan for another 90-day action plan.

REVIEWS

Plans and their progress should be regularly reviewed to ensure everyone, yourself included, is on course. Use the flexibility within plans to fine-tune them as you progress. The frequency of reviews depends on the individual. Disciplined people will need fewer reviews than less-focused, poorly disciplined people.

It is a common error to confuse activity with accomplishment and think we are doing all the right things, when in fact we are going nowhere. Seek support from your upline to ensure you are using the right materials, saying the right things and making the proper impact on your prospects to make them want to join your team.

Timing of plans

The implementation of a plan gets everyone started on their first steps of the ladder to success. It takes courage to put a plan into action and you must consider carefully when to introduce a plan to new team members.

It is a mistake to expect all new people to be ready to take a plan forward immediately. "But", you say, "Isn't that why they joined the business in the first place?" Yes, but everyone's bedding-in period is different. They feel the need to establish their belief and understanding, when we know that if they just get on with the job the belief and understanding will come spontaneously.

If you confront them with a plan too quickly, before they have had time to settle into the business, they may not be ready to accept it. It takes different people different amounts of time to establish their belief. It may be after they have attended a couple of events, or have met a leader who can settle their concerns. We must respect each individual.

A friend who had been in networking for some years had taken several steps up the marketing plan, when BOOM!......His business exploded, growing faster in the following two years than it had done in the previous five. When we asked what had changed, his reply was – 'The timing was right for me. I've had a lot to cope with in my personal life, but I just kept my business ticking over, knowing that the time would come when I would be ready to take it forward'. Now his business has a regular monthly turnover of £millions.

No one, in any network marketing company, has so good a team that it cannot be improved by sponsoring another ten new people. If you did this today imagine how fast your business would grow, followed closely by the welcome exponential growth in income.

So commit once more to the system, revisit your strict personal activity plan, and take action to find them. Lead by example, get cracking on your lead generation activity and sponsor these ten new people. If your team do the same, imagine the excitement and momentum it will bring.

Ye Olde saying:

'If you fail to plan

You plan to fail'

Mistakes and Lessons

Mistake no 1

Over the years we have heard many people declare: 'I am serious about my business, I'm working on my plan every day'. Their fatal mistake is 'working on their plan every day' instead of taking action to complete the tasks to 'work their plan'. They are the ones who spend time projecting figures, shuffling paper work, tidying their desks, getting their office ready to 'get serious'. They confuse these activities with business building activity.

Lesson no 1

When you work from home people don't believe you have a proper job. It's assumed you can help with the school run, take neighbours to the doctor, help out with the shopping etc. So make your business plan and make it clear to everyone that you are 'in business'.

Mistake no 2

Pushing people too hard too early; wanting them to succeed in the business more than they want to themselves.

Lesson no 2

Keep exposing them to positive material and messages and sooner or later something will 'flick their switch'. Try not to become frustrated, especially when you know they have the potential to succeed.

It takes everyone a different amount of time to grasp what they can really achieve, and to understand how much time they need to set aside to complete their business plan.

Meanwhile, you must always keep focused on your own plans.

Chapter 11

The Numbers Game

"The Numbers Game"

Playing the numbers game is just like putting fuel in your car. If you don't put the fuel in you won't get very far – it's the same in any network marketing business.

We are amazed how many people we meet who do not have a sponsoring or lead generating plan in place as part of their team building activity. A new person starting out to build a team must have a crystal clear plan of action to take them to the first serious position in the marketing plan.

There is a temptation to try to force plans upon new distributors. We find that most new people need a bedding-in period, time to get familiar with the system and grasp a basic understanding of the whole concept. Some people take longer than others and during this period gentle, encouraging communication is required. It is part of what we refer to as baby sitting; helping new distributors to move some products, getting them along to events, and starting on voice mail or conference calls. In short, anything that will help them see the 'bigger picture'. We use any tool which will inspire, educate and motivate our new people to make a start on their business building activities.

A common mistake made by new people occurs when their first five or six prospects don't join. Their enthusiasm dwindles or, worse still, they stop playing the numbers game before they have even completed the first round.

FOCUS ON THE ACTIVITIES AND
THE RESULTS WILL LOOK AFTER THEMSELVES

If you are sending out information packs or email packs you must do enough lead generating activity to create enough leads to have an effect. Sending out only one or two packs per week, or making two or three phone calls to people you know to arrange meetings, is too small a number.

Whatever the system your successful upline uses and teaches, team building relies on the numbers game. Learn how to -

Use it
Understand it
Accept it and
Get on with it

Over time and with persistent, consistent practice your lead generating activity will become more and more effective.

Every person who says 'no' takes you closer to the ones who will say 'yes'.

Remember that when someone says 'no', they are saying 'no' to the business, not to yourself; so don't take a rejection personally.

Take 'no' as meaning 'not right now, thank you'.

Keep the lines of communication open, because in most peoples' lives timing is a key factor. You can revisit the 'no' prospects at a later date. They will have moved on and may be more receptive next time round.

When playing the numbers game don't put too much reliance on any one person. Don't concentrate on one prospect to the exclusion of others. The purpose of playing the numbers game is to inform as many prospects as possible about your business and the opportunity you are offering them. After you have given a business presentation, shown an e-brochure or sent your information -

> THE FORTUNE IS FOUND IN THE FOLLOW UP

We have watched people do perfect presentations, faithfully following their successful upline's methods, but still struggle to have anyone join their team. The miracle part of playing the numbers game is ALWAYS in the follow up.

It is most unlikely that prospects will call you back after a presentation, no matter what they say or how impressed they are. You MUST follow up your prospect within a maximum of 48 hours of making your pitch.

Our experience has been that if we leave it any longer, the 'negatrons' will get to them. These are negative people who influence other people's success. You can never be sure where they will turn up. But they are out there and you may even be sleeping with one! Negatives creep in and create self-doubts, and your prospect can be lost forever.

You can show people a brilliant opportunity, an opportunity that can truly change their lives, an opportunity to create a lifestyle that most people scarcely know exists. Yet your prospect can, and will, listen to people who know nothing about your business or industry, people who struggle daily to make ends meet.

The Excellent Prospect

I remember meeting an excellent prospect - although he was rather young. He had his goals mapped out, which was quite unusual for someone so young. He was totally positive about the idea of having his own business and paid great attention to my presentation, following it with some first-rate questions, which I answered thoroughly. He went away very happy, with the information pack and DVD, saying he would call me the following day.

As we part from any prospect we always say - 'If I don't hear from you, I will call you in the next couple of days. Is that OK? (We always ask, "Is that OK?", as we have then asked their permission to call them back).

Needless to say he didn't call. When I called him two days later he sounded a bit downhearted. I asked how he felt about our business and network marketing, had he watched the DVD and did he have any further questions? He replied that he was no longer interested as his mother said that she didn't think it would work!

Having heard similar replies many times before, I continued: "With greatest respect to your mother, may I ask what she does for a living? Is she in business for herself and is she qualified to make that statement? We must respect other people's opinions, but as one of our respected leaders says: 'We should never be influenced by others' well-meaning, but uninformed, opinions'".

It turned out that his dear mother was a cleaner at the local bingo hall!

It is very sad that people can be robbed of the fantastic opportunity you offer them because they listen to good-intentioned, but totally ill-informed, opinions. The only thing you can do is make sure that they have your contact details in case they should change their minds in the future. It may help them to do so if you feed them new success stories now and again.

Your Sponsoring Plan

> Networking is a people game.
> If you have no prospects for the future,
> you have no future prospects.

Do not exclude anyone from your personal contact list. We cannot advocate this strongly enough, as none of us wants anyone to come to a meeting or training night and find that their best friend has been invited by someone else! Let everyone know about your new business. Tell everybody how excited you are about your new career, and tell them to tell their own friends.

When building your contact list don't wait until you have 100's of names to start contacting prospects. Your list should be a 'work in progress' tool. As soon as you have details for the first ten or fifteen prospects, get started playing the numbers game. As you tick off names you have contacted you should be adding more to replace them.

Structure your sponsoring/lead generation plan sensibly, especially if you are part-time. Commit to doing 1, 2 or 3 calls per day. Too often people get over-enthusiastic and say, "I'll do 10 a day". Most people don't have time for 10 calls and quickly find it unsustainable, and as a result lose heart.

Your plan must be sustainable. Two calls per day for the next five years is more realistic than 100 calls this week. There will be exceptions to this, like ourselves; we didn't have time to wait and increased our lead generation activity to achieve a goal of ten appointments a day.

> Your plan should be,
> to realistically do
> what you can sustain
> in order to create your required momentum.

The top scorer in any football team is usually the player who has also had most misses. He doesn't score every time he shoots for goal, but he makes more opportunities to do so than anyone else in his team. It's just another way of expressing the numbers game. Every miss takes the footballer closer to scoring a goal.

Likewise your own success will come from being the best player at the numbers game. Every prospect who says 'no' takes you closer to the prospect who says 'yes'.

Each time you get ready to play the numbers game, before you pick up the telephone, before presenting your business to a prospect, try the following exercise.

Cover the mouths in the diagram with a piece of paper. Look closely at the eyes in each face, they all look the same. Remove the paper. Now look again and see how the eyes change in each one.

Which face would you like to be associated with? – obviously number 3. Everyone likes to see a smiling face. Before you dial your next prospect, remember the eyes. Have a smile on your face and a smile in your voice. People can tell, even over the phone, if you are smiling or not.

This exercise demonstrates how very important it is to learn to be the person whose team people want to join. Avoid fake enthusiasm; be genuinely excited about your company, your business and your goals. Someone said – 'A smile is the thin line that can make all the difference'.

If you are not enthusiastic about your business you can't expect other people to be either.

Ye Olde Saying:

SW SW SW SW

Some Will

Some Won't

So What

Someone (is) Waiting

Mistakes and Lessons

Mistake no. 1
Stopping playing the numbers game after only a few telephone calls because you don't get a result.

Lesson no. 1
Understand the concept of playing the numbers game. Ask, ask, ask your upline if you are not having success with your phone calls. Your system should teach you how to best approach prospects.

Mistake no. 2

Working in spurts of activity and failing to generate enough leads consistently.

Lesson no. 2

This is a very common problem and causes the loss of all the momentum you have created. People falling into this trap see their turnover decrease and become depressed. To avoid this mistake stick firmly to your weekly sponsoring/lead generating plan. Keep in regular contact with your successful upline at all times.

Chapter 12

Your Friend The Telephone

"fear of the phone"

What's your telephone? Ours is just that extension to our arms that we happen to talk into. It links our living room to our friends and relations, and we chat away to each other sixteen-to-the-dozen and never give a thought that there's tens, hundreds or maybe thousands of miles between us in our virtual telephone world. It's OK, isn't it, when we're talking to our best friends; we take it all for granted and forget the phone even is there.

But when it's 'The Telephone in The Office' it turns into a bit of a beast! No, not really. It's just another plastic gizmo that's indispensable to businesses, and to businessmen and business women who have a vision of where they want to get to.

We look back to when we started in this industry. We followed the instructions of our successful upline, wrote down our lists of prospects and researched the telephone numbers. Then it was time to make the phone calls.

We knew that if we were to build a team, the calls had to be made. After a typical husband and wife 'discussion', John was nominated to make the first call to our first prospect. We agreed what he would say, then he had to pick up the telephone.

Nervously he picked it up and dialled the number, saying "This man will be a superstar in our team, I just know it". He let the phone ring twice, slammed it back on the receiver and announced –"He's not in". I replied, "Maybe he's not standing right next to the phone, waiting for you to call offering him a fantastic life changing opportunity. Give him a chance to answer this time".

Plucking up courage a second time John redialled and let it ring six or seven times, and slammed the handset down again, announcing, "See, I told you, he's not in". Moments later our telephone rang. It was the early days of the 1471 telephone redial service and this was our prospect calling us back. John was so taken aback when he answered that he couldn't admit to the prospect the real reason for phoning, and arranged a game of squash with him instead!

It was fear, that existed only in John's mind, that was holding him back.

When we do anything new it always feels awkward and everyone is affected differently. Don't worry; it's a perfectly natural human reaction. You're not the first person to feel this way, and you certainly won't be the last.

We always made our calls together; one made the call while the other listened. This way we could help each other improve with constructive criticism. When we recall what we said on some of those early phone calls we wonder how we ever got some of the appointments, but we did.

Our script wasn't perfect and we said things we knew we shouldn't. But the point was, we made the calls. We took the necessary action we knew would bring results. And we held our telephoning sessions when the children weren't about, so that there would be no interruptions or distractions. These were important business calls; the calls that would lead to appointments and people joining our team.

Practise makes Perfect

The telephone is only a beast if you allow it to be. It's all in your imagination. Now John is an expert on the telephone. He sometimes comes off a call saying it went so well he feels like signing himself up all over again.

He has overcome his fears and gained confidence by practice, consistently maintaining his daily, weekly, monthly telephone activity, always striving to improve his technique and success rate. He makes live phone calls at trainings before audiences of 30-40 people, leading by example and achieving results with total confidence.

The more calls you make the sooner the fear and awkwardness disappear. The more preparation and practice you do, the better you become. Before you know it, it has become second nature.

Use a telephone script. Type out your upline's proven successful script and have it on the desk in front of you, especially when you are new and nervous. Scripts are tried and tested and an invaluable tool to help you overcome your nervousness and gain confidence and telephone skills.

Phone Tips

Different leaders use different phone techniques and phone scripts. Find the ones that work best and use them.

1) Learn to listen well – if you ask enough questions, and ask the right questions, your prospect will give you a lead how best to grab their attention or hit their 'hot buttons'.

2) Tell your prospect only enough to sharpen their interest and get them to the next stage, whether it's to arrange a 1-to-1 presentation or send out information.

3) For close friends or family, don't use the phone scripts, simply say - "Hi, it's me. Get the kettle on, I'm coming round. I've something to show you that I'm really excited about. I can't tell you on the phone, I need to show you".

4) Objections are good - it shows that your prospects are interested. So expect objections and be ready to respond to them. Don't try to evade objections, and the

more successfully you learn to deal with them the more confident you will become.

5) Always be truthful. Admit it if you don't know the answer to a question. No one expects you to know everything, so say that you will call back when you have the answer.

6) Don't let your phone call develop into an argument. You can win an argument but you may lose the battle and alienate your prospect for ever. Keep your lines of communication open so you can re-contact the prospect later. Timing can change people's point of view.

To help handle objections and avoid arguments we use an old networking favourite: Feel, Felt, and Found.

> I know how you feel,
> I felt the same, until
> I found out.....

Release Statements

Use what we call 'release statements' at the end of the call. We use them to summarise our discussion, to reassure prospects and release them from any pressure.

For instance, after arranging an appointment tell your prospect what will happen at your meeting. Give your prospect a summary – "We will meet for a coffee, and I will run the business past you properly. I'll answer all your personal questions, and give you information to take away with you so that you can make an informed decision.

Or, after arranging to send out information – "I will send you a brochure and a DVD today which you should receive tomorrow. I'll call you in two days to allow you time to watch the DVD and read the information, then I can answer all your questions."

Once you have met your prospects, or they have read your information, it is vital to contact them again within 48 hours. As we have said in the chapter entitled 'The Numbers Game' –

THE FORTUNE IS IN THE FOLLOW UP

Ye Olde saying:

'Learn to say less to more people'

Mistakes and Lessons

<u>Mistake no 1</u>
Making too few phone calls to generate any momentum.

<u>Lesson no 1</u>
It takes consistency to build a business, which means doing enough lead generation activity to keep you persistently on the

phone. If your phone calls are meeting with little or no success – stop. Ask your upline for help, use three-way calling.

<u>Mistake no 2</u>
Saying too much on the telephone.

<u>Lesson no 2</u>
Think what the aim is of the phone call to a new prospect. It's not to sell the sausage, sizzle and all. It's to get your prospect to the next stage, whether it is an appointment or sending out information. Prospects don't need to know every percentage figure, or how the company marketing plan works or how bonuses are calculated. That is the reason you want to meet, or send them information. Giving too much information too early merely gives your prospect opportunities for objections and reasons not to join your business.

Make the phone your friend .

Chapter 13

Presenting Your Business

Simplicity is the key to presentations

Presenting your business to prospects who have shown interest in network marketing is a critical stage in building your business. It is an ongoing part of the system which must be visited daily to ensure that your team numbers are not only maintained, but that they increase. People quit the business for all sorts of reasons, and if you fail to anticipate this in the early days you could find that your only team member is yourself!

We meet prospects in hotels, or invite them to our home if they live nearby. When we first started our business we certainly didn't invite people to our home. The last place we wanted prospects to meet us was in the rundown cottage we were living in.

That was part of our strong 'WHY' to make our business work – to get out of the horrible situation we found ourselves living in. How could we show people a business that could make them rich and set them free, while we were living in accommodation that did not portray that image? We are very happy now to invite people to our very nice house.

The reason we meet people in our home or in hotels is simple - we need to be able to control the environment in order to control the meeting. The purpose of the meeting is to present the benefits of a professional business and our time is extremely valuable - so we don't want distractions.

You are offering a genuine professional business opportunity and you need your prospect's attention throughout. How can you show people what a fantastic financial future they can provide for themselves and their family, if their attention is distracted by their children or the family pets demanding attention, the background noise of television, music or the telephone ringing?

Get your prospect away from his or her familiar environment where family priorities cannot intrude. If a prospect were applying for a position within a conventional company they would not be interviewed in their own home.

Preparation

You only have one chance to make a first impression. Be professional and businesslike at all times. Dress smartly; put on a suit, or at least a jacket, and wear a tie. Have clean shoes and tidy hair.

Start with your personal preparation time before you leave your home, office or work place. Ensure you have all the tools you will need for the presentation; the tools you will use and the tools you will give your prospect to take away after the presentation.
You are about to give a presentation on a business idea that can change a person's life and future, so look the part and be prepared.

The Presentation

Remember your objective with the presentation. It is an introductory presentation and you are there only to inform, not to impress. The purpose of the meeting is to show your prospect a brief overview of the business opportunity you are offering, and what it can do for them. You are selling the sizzle and not the sausage. Answer their questions and give them more information to take away for further reading.

We always start with a friendly conversation to relax prospects - asking questions about themselves, their work or family. Everyone's best topic of conversation is themselves, so try to relate to your prospect. If you learn to ask the right questions they will actually tell you how to sponsor them. Learn to be a good listener, saying less and listening more. Remember, we have two ears and one mouth; use them in that ratio.

We have many examples of people who typify the saying 'a little knowledge is a dangerous thing'. These are distributors starting to build a new team who are carried away with their own ingenuity. In their efforts to show how clever and knowledgeable they are they use industry jargon and 'in house' language and terminology. And they carry this into their introductory presentations.

They confuse prospects with facts and figures and unnecessary diagrams. They convey the impression that one needs to be an industry expert to even consider joining the company, and that is the impression the prospect goes away with. Think about your own experience: if you don't understand something how often do you buy it?

> THE MOMENT YOU BECOME COMPLICATED YOU BECOME INEFFECTUAL.

Your presentation must be kept simple and straightforward. If prospects are to have the confidence to join your business, they need to see that they can do the job that you are doing. Duplication is the key; use the brochures and tools that your successful upline promotes to illustrate the system you are following.

We show prospects the kind of people who get involved in our industry and what they have achieved. They see that they are people just like themselves. We briefly explain the company background and the potential benefits which the company offers them. Mentally we are showing them how the system can work for them and how they can earn money.

Go into these introductory presentations with the mindset that it's not what you can get out of the meeting, it's what the meeting can do for the prospect, and how you can help your prospect to achieve. Always aim to communicate, rather than conduct a lecture which is a one-way conversation. Make sure the prospect feels comfortable, physically as well as mentally. Ask questions all the time, so that they feel involved. "Are you with me so far?", "Do you have any questions?", "Have I explained this sufficiently?", "Is that OK?"

Don't overcomplicate the issue at this early stage. Provide a brief description or overview of the marketing plan and how it can work for them – mentally putting the money in their pocket. Show your prospect some success stories which reinforce how the marketing plan works and how it can work for them. Show examples of high earnings and successful life styles. This is the information which best illustrates the potential of the opportunity you are holding out.

You must include in your presentation details of the initial registration or start-up costs involved. You will have explained that everyone joining your company is being offered the chance to have, run and own their own business, so obviously there must be a cost involved. Clearly explain your company's options which will illustrate that the initial outlay is low.

Be honest at all times, and finish off with a brief summary highlighting the benefits of becoming part of your business.

Then leave; don't get yourself into a situation where the prospect may go back to the beginning

In our experience a good presentation should last about forty minutes, but no longer than an hour and a half – it depends on the prospect. Even in this day and age of electronic communication we believe that our business is built on relationships. Your presentation is the start of what could be a mutually profitable relationship. It takes about twenty minutes to describe the real potential of our business, and the rest of the time is spent communicating and connecting with your prospect. In fact we believe that creating empathy can be as persuasive a factor in getting them on board with you, as it is them grasping the potential of the business.

People forget what you say, but they never forget how you made them feel.
Don't give lectures, learn to listen and answer questions. When you are finished, leave them the additional information you brought. If you are in doubt, consult with your successful upline what materials you should leave with prospects.

Ye Olde saying:
'The Speed of the Team
Is Set by
The Speed of the Leader'

118

Mistakes and Lessons

Mistake no. 1
Information overload!

Lesson no. 1
Know when to stop your presentation. Don't 'ever-egg the cake' during it. Don't talk prospects in and then talk them out again. Answer all their questions, but give them only enough information to want to get involved and move to the next step on your business plan.

Mistake no.2
There are plenty examples of new leaders who, having introduced three or four new people, let their momentum slide and appear to think they need do no more. They stop presentations and sending out information packs.

Lesson no. 2
Make sure you always maintain your lead generating activity.

Chapter 14

The Power of a Testimonial

'Importance of Testimonials'

People underestimate how powerful personal testimonials are in this industry. Their primary aim was originally thought to be for the benefit of the new people in the room, still just looking at the business. But they serve more than one purpose, and what we have found over the years is that testimonials can motivate and inspire everyone.

The most excited person in the room is the new person who has just achieved his or her first success. Don't underestimate the power of your story, even if it's your first week in your new business and you don't think your achievement is in the least significant. A result of any description is a result, be it a first small cheque, or you have moved some product, or you have just signed up your first prospect. Be proud of your result no matter how small it may appear.

The aim of having testimonials at meetings by people from different backgrounds and at different positions in the marketing plan, is to relate to as many of the audience as possible. Be it a new person looking at the business for the first time, or an experienced distributor, every testimonial has a message that can help you build your business.

Like relates to like

If you have a prospect or new team member who is, say, a schoolteacher, introduce them to a schoolteacher who is already in your team. Your team schoolteacher will encourage the newcomer and explain how to fit their networking business in with their daily schedule.

Giving a testimonial before an audience for the first time can be overwhelming. John's biggest fear was public speaking and his first testimonial was unforgettable. Up till then I had given 'our' testimonials.

A few weeks earlier we had met a very successful distributor who had taken a great interest in us and later became a great friend and mentor. He explained to John, "If you want success in this industry you need to be at the front of the room, holding the pen. If you are going to be the leader, you need to lead from the front of the room".

This was like a body blow to John and he had sleepless nights before the event at which he was to make his public speaking debut. Just before the testimonials started he excused himself, saying he had to leave the room. He locked himself in the toilet until the meeting was finished.

Open nights were held monthly and John was determined to overcome his fear, promising that he would make his contribution next month. He prepared and practised his first big speech, which was to last only 60 seconds.

At our next local open night the host announced, "And now we'll hear from John Stephen". When John stood up his brain sat down. He lost his power of speech momentarily, and when he did eventually mumble a few words he had forgotten what he was going to say; he couldn't even remember his name. It was terrible, but it was enough to have faced his fear, and soon he was giving testimonials without a backward thought.

When he stands up now, sometimes in front of audiences of thousands, people can scarcely believe that story. We are now both honoured and delighted when we are asked to give talks and lead trainings all over the country. It demonstrates how developing your ability at public speaking is part of getting involved and becoming part of the system.

<u>How to Give a Testimonial</u>

A testimonial should be short and to the point.
1) Name and Background
2) When and Why you joined
3) What you have achieved / What you enjoy / What has helped you most

Avoid using jargon or in-house terminology in your testimonial. Remember, if you have reached a position in your marketing plan such as Direct Distributor, Executive Sales Leader or Executive Distributor this means nothing to the new people. It's the same if you have percentage positions in your company and you make statements such as – "I've now reached 20%". This means nothing to new people and the people you are trying to relate to.

Practice testimonials in front of the mirror, or before a member of your family. The more competent your performance the better you will look in front of your team and the prospects at the meeting. A testimonial is not for 'selling' or delivering a personal training, it is to relate to the people in the audience.

How Not To Give A Testimonial

A 'memorable' testimonial was given by a person who told us his name and that he was born by caesarean section; he listed the schools he had attended and all the jobs he had had, and much more. To crown it all he announced to the meeting that his beautiful wife had just conceived with the aid of IVF test tube technology. While everyone was very happy for him and his pregnant wife, none of it had any relevance to a testimonial about his new business.

A testimonial is not your life's history, its purpose is to relate to others in the audience and demonstrate Who and What and Why has contributed to your achievements. Keeping your testimonial related to your business will motivate and inspire others.

One thing we have found out to be true is that FEAR is -

F - False
E - Evidence
A - Appearing
R - Real

When it is time to give your testimonial the only place that fear exists is in your mind. When you hear John giving a training, and he speaks about fear, you will know he has truly experienced it. The other more experienced distributors will also know how you feel. If they know it is your first attempt at public speaking you can be sure they are just as nervous for you, as you are feeling yourself.

It is inspiring to see people standing in front of an audience, addressing a meeting and giving testimonials and trainings, and remembering how they started years earlier. We know they have worked on their personal development and practised to become the person 'at the front of the room holding the pen'.

They are the leaders of the future.

Chapter 15

The Final Chapter

"I'm not good enough to try that yet", or "I don't have enough experience yet". We've heard those fears so often. But don't lose heart, we know how you feel. Indeed, we felt the same until we found out that a job worth doing, is worth doing badly until you have practised and gained the experience to do it well.

When we look back to where we were when we entered this industry many years ago, we know we are a million miles away from that point today. We could never have imagined writing one book, never mind writing a second one and producing a CD called 'Starting your Success'.

When we signed the application forms to join our company we little imagined the lifestyle we have today. The holidays and experiences we have enjoyed with friends and family in every corner of the world were just pipe dreams then. We have made valued and lasting friendships within our own team and company and within the industry as a whole. And it gives us daily pleasure to anticipate the lifestyle that we believe our two amazing teenagers are sure to have. It has come from the positive attitudes and wisdom which we have gained as we built our business, and which we have been able to pass on to them.

> We discovered that if we wanted things
> we had never had before,
> we needed to do things
> we had never done before.

When you get comfortable with being uncomfortable, that's when you have pushed yourself beyond the limits of your comfort zone. You've expanded it by breaking new boundaries and before long, as a matter of routine, you are doing new tasks that once you feared. To get where we are today we have continually expanded the boundaries of our individual and joint comfort zones. That didn't happen by accident.

Will Success Come for you?

Success comes by taking the time to learn the system and following your successful upline. Commit to your company's programme until you reach the level of success you desire. When you work on your personal development programme, through time you will see yourself reaching the goals you once could only have dreamed about.

Hold fast to your belief that you will achieve your goals and dreams. Have confidence that you can, and will, climb your ladder of belief and become a successful leader in the network marketing industry.

The dream is there if you are willing to change and work hard to achieve success. With every step you climb of your company's marketing plan you can see far enough ahead to get you to the next step, and so on, step by step, until you reach the top. But first you must aim for that first step. If your success is slow in coming, be flexible and start a new 90-day action plan with renewed vigour, new motivation, and new understanding. You can succeed just as we have done.

What needs to be done today?

Take ownership of your business. We said at the start of this book – YOU are the business owner. Be proud of the industry you have joined for it can give you a future other people only dream of. You can have it all – start today by taking responsibility for your success. Work your successful upline's system and learn to use each part.

Take Action Today

A great feature of owning a network marketing business is that you can start again today. Whether you are starting out for the first time today, or you have lost direction and grown stale, you can start a 90-day action plan with fresh attitude and enthusiasm. In a conventional business this sort of situation could cost you everything.

How It Really Works

We included 'How it really works' in the title of this book because we know network marketing works. In our years in the industry we have seen it work for many others. We have experienced the ups and downs, the positives and negatives and are more excited today about the industry than we have ever been.

Network marketing still works and it will continue to do so. Regardless of developments in communications and technology (which we embrace) we believe that business today, and in the future, will be built more and more on relationships. Network marketing is a people business and the synergy of relationships is the life-blood of the industry.

Can It Work for You?

We honestly believe that network marketing can work for you no matter what your previous experience or background. It gives you the opportunity to create a new future and lifestyle for yourself and your family, and to become financially independent with a business which, if managed correctly, will give you everything you can ever dream of.

Take advice from your successful upline; become the most teachable person you know; don't fall into the Mistake no.1 trap referred to in Chapter 1 –' What is there to learn?' Be wise and be honest with yourself and recognise that you have a lot to learn in your network marketing business, not just today but for years to come. But always believe that it can work for you.

We are in the final chapter and we have not yet mentioned passion. Develop a passion for your success. A passion for the industry you have chosen to become part of, and a passion to help other people succeed. Only by helping others can you truly succeed yourself.

You need your passion to drive you to do the daily activities which move you closer to your WHY? Finding your WHY? will move you forward to make a plan. Stick to your plan and take the correct actions. Re-read the Mistakes and Lessons in each chapter of this book. Avoiding the mistakes and learning the lessons will speed you forward to achieving your dreams and goals.

Ye Olde Saying:

'Ignorance on Fire

is better than

Knowledge on Ice'

We truly hope that you take and apply the knowledge you have gained from this book, and that you do what has to be done to become the person who deserves your WHY?

We can wish you success with your network marketing business, but our good wishes won't bring you your success.

Only you can find your passion.
Only you can find your WHY?
Only you can be the one
who ultimately decides if
you will or will not be successful.

John & Hazel

(**PLEASE NOTE: None of the information or companies below promote any specific Network Marketing Programme)

To order more copies of this book visit:

www.jandhproductions.com

Also available to order 'Where Does It All Start?' Personal Development book and 'Starting Your Success' CD.

Full size forms from this book available for free download at the above web site.

Other Useful Links:

www.lifestylearchitecture.co.uk

www.thewebcrew.com

www.knowledgeisking.co.uk

www.mlmmessaging.com